Ele-Mental

Hayley Lazzari

Volume 1

Spinning Monkey Press | Keene

Spinning Monkey Press LLC
196 Main Street #547
Keene, NH 03431
www.spinningmonkeypress.com

Publisher's Note: This is a work of fiction. Names, characters, places, and incidents are a product of the author's imagination. Locales and public names are sometimes used for atmospheric purposes. Any resemblance to actual people, living or dead, or to businesses, companies, events, institutions, or locales is completely coincidental.

Cover Design by Marta Susic Obucina

Ele-Mental Vol. 1/ Hayley Lazzari. -- 1st ed.
ISBN 979-8-9857695-2-4

To Alex, Bex, and Collin
The beginning of my alphabet
And my home when I needed one most
Your love saves my life every day
And I'll spend the rest of mine showing you
how grateful I am
Until EE

Contents

ELE-MENTAL

Preface

In April 2022, after suffering with mental illness for over 15 years, a dozen ER visits for suicidal ideation, and three ambulance trips, I found myself in a psych ward. Over the course of three separate hospitalizations in the same year, I spent a total of 25 days in psych units. Before being committed, I had only ever experienced a psych ward through the lens of television and novels. Of course, the exaggerated nature of fiction had me terrified of what was to come after being admitted. I wasn't prepared for the love, acceptance, camaraderie, and laughs that came during the next few weeks. While I was there, I was fortunate enough to meet people who have become close friends. On the other hand, I also suffered all of the trauma that comes with such an ordeal – fights, alarms, being woken at all hours of the night, room checks, screaming, etc. In short, it was probably the most difficult thing I've ever had to go through, but it also saved my life.

I won't bore you with the details of my diagnoses or the tedium of everyday life on the ward, but I will tell you that a psych ward is likely the most misunderstood ecosystem in our society. Where the media would show you strait jackets and padded rooms, I found a place where people were just people. Yes, we were suffering in different ways and that suffering was expressed in many fashions (for better or for worse), but we were also just seen as humans instead of "the crazy person" or "the weird kid." We played Uno and Jenga; the food wasn't terrible; and we laughed, cried, and talked. My goal isn't to romanticize an in-patient program – there is nothing romantic or beautiful about it – but I'd like to humanize it. I was extremely sick before entering the psych ward, and in a lot of ways, it didn't prepare me for going back into my real life, but I'm grateful that it gave me a chance.

After leaving the hospital for the second time, I entered a partial hospitalization program (PHP).

During the following six weeks, I spent the equivalent of 9-5 in the hospital attending group sessions for trauma management, music therapy, poetry, coping with stress, art, individual therapy sessions, and dozens of other things. At first, I felt like a child or an invalid, but the third floor quickly became a safe haven. In all the ways that the psych ward was safe, the PHP program was better. We all had varied in-patient experiences and wanted to avoid going back at all costs. We appreciated that no one would judge us within the walls of the third floor, and we always had each other's backs. Friendships blossomed for me there as well with people of all ages and origins. Pick-up basketball became the highlight of my weeks. However, I was still struggling. I almost committed suicide on several occasions. I had issues with drinking and drugs. Worst of all, I wasn't sure how to talk to my friends "on the outside" – I still don't. I feel as if my mental illnesses have caused a chasm to open up, and I am suddenly on the other side. This, along with a lot of other things, is something I'm continuing to work on. I'm still healing and growing and hurting, and I will be for a long time.

I say all of this not to elicit pity or tell you my sob story. This is simply the backdrop against which I wrote this book. Every word was written over the course of the several months I spent in hospitals and psych wards. Poetry became the method through which I came to express myself most authentically and most honestly. I hope that my words make you feel *something* – positive, negative, or somewhere in between. I leave my heart in your hands. Thanks for reading!

Part I: Water
On Memory

What horror
Must be left behind
To be unable to trust
Your own memory,
Recollecting
Only embers
From a fire burnt long ago
I can smell the flame
Licking at charred wood
I can feel the heat,
The smoke in my lungs,
But they tell me
There was no blaze,
That my mind
Is playing tricks
On me –
Like every day is April 1st
And I'm the butt
Of every joke
But if there was no inferno
Why do I have
Third degree burns?

I don't know what to believe – and other
tragedies

A memory
Within a memory,
Within a memory,
Thoughts lost
In the optical illusion
My brain insists on
Creating,
Circling round and round –
A fractal with no end.
It makes me dizzy,
Nauseated,
Digging through
The gray matter,
Searching for something
That feels real, concrete
Instead of a wisp of smoke
Caught by the wind
Before I can inhale it,
Frantic
About the stretches of black
I cannot fill
But then I stop
And rest
And think that perhaps
I have a guardian angel
Shielding me from things
It knows
I should not know

A protector – and a saboteur

If the Big Bad Wolf
Came knocking on my past,
He'd huff
And he'd puff,
And he'd blow
The sawdust
I mistake for memories
To bits

Remnants – of whatever destroyed the evidence

When I was small,
I was afraid of the dark,
Scared of finding
Monsters in my closet,
In my dreams,
Terrified of the unknown.
But I've since learned
That the real monsters
Live in my head,
In my veins,
And don't always keep
To the shadows of night.
Sometimes
They make you
Wish for never-ending darkness,
Even as the sun shines
Through the windows
And doors
Of every place you've ever known

I'm the monster – and other sad truths

I think often of my father,
5'11 and full of rage;
How the air used to radiate
Around him,
Palpable with temper
With stress.
I think often of my father
And how much of him
I carry with me
Every day,
How heavy he has made my life
Without even knowing
He has been force-feeding me rocks
Since the day I was born.
I think often of my father
And how I will never measure up
To his version of perfect,
But as long as I never
Look in the mirror
And see my father
Staring back at me,
I'll consider myself
Perfect enough

What he doesn't know – almost broke me

I think often of my mother
And the river of tears
I have seen her shed
To bear the burden
Of being.
I think often of my mother
And the fury
That used to scare me
But I now understand
Better than I wish to.
I think often of my mother,
Who I was too young
To save
And who was too broken
To save me.
I think often of my mother
And how glad I am
We have each other,
How lucky I am
It wasn't too late
For us to be friends

You can choose your friends – but not your
family

At 16 years old,
I taped
Poorly constructed
Print outs
Of my favorite quotes –
Dark, despondent lines
Describing secrets
And scars
And methods
To eviscerate one's mind
To keep the pain at bay –
To the mirror
Above my dresser
In a neat little grid
Under the medals and ribbons –
Props for the role
I felt compelled to play.
In December
Of that year,
I caught my mother
Reading them
As I hid behind the corner,
Out of sight
And watched her
Walk away,
Never asking
If I was okay,
Never asking
If I needed help
And so I assumed
That I was fine

How was I supposed to know – and other core
memories

Success
Has always been defined for me
Without my consent,
Using euphemisms
For impossible expectations
Like
A college degree
From a "good school,"
"Respectable" job,
Six figure salary,
2.5 kids,
White picket fence,
Things meant to build a life
That they'll inevitably destroy.
They don't care
About that part;
They won't help you
If you fall.
All that matters is
The perception
Of success,
The façade
Of happiness,
Which is why
I am lying in a hospital bed
Wishing I were dead

What else was I supposed to do – it must be my
fault

They built me
Of their mistakes
And were surprised
When I couldn't survive

What did they expect – besides the impossible

Out!
The word rips
Across the stadium,
A vicious wind
Producing cheers
Or jeers
Depending on
The color of your jersey.
It's innocuous,
A necessity
At a baseball game
But now
I'm far away
Drawing myself
Away from the friends
Who think I don't notice
When they exchange glances
And texts
When I'm not looking,
And soon I'm lost
In my memory
Where out
Means something
Very different

I'm out - of my mind

I didn't know
I was abused
Until I was several states away,
Flinching
Every time someone
Tried to touch me
And feeling panicked
When no one punished
My imperfections.
I still don't quite know
What abuse means
To me;
I still don't know
How much it
Changed me;
I still don't know
Everything I went through,
But I do know
That some things
Are better
Lost in time

Abuse is an ugly word – but it doesn't make it
untrue

Your skin
On my skin
Should be a relief,
An island paradise
In an unforgiving ocean.
Instead
Being naked
And feeling your hands
Inside me,
Your tongue
Mingling with mine
Has my heart racing
In time to your rhythm
And suddenly
I'm no longer there.
The college dive
I knew well enough to avoid
Is blurry in the background,
214 miles away
But right next door.
He's breathing down my neck,
Asking me to dance,
And then we're
Outside,
Stumbling through the snow,
His arm around my shoulders,
Clouds of hot air
And the footprints left behind
The only evidence
We were here.
His room is dark, dirty,
But I feel dirtier

As he whispers all the things
He wants to do to me.
My vision is swimming
"Can I take the condom off?"
As if I knew he was inside me
"You were the best fuck I've had"
Reducing me to a conquest
As if I should be proud
Of the pleasure I gave him
But never consented to.
The alcohol humming in my veins;
I forget my shirt,
I forget my name.
Back out into the snow
What time is it?
My hallway is empty,
But at least the lights are on
I'm afraid of the dark
Sitting on the floor of the bathroom,
Blood seeping into my underwear,
Bruises on my neck,
Back against the door –
To keep people out
Or seal me in,
I'm not sure.
Darkness will give way to morning
And maybe this won't be real
"Are you okay?"
Snapping back to your voice,
Your hands,
Your lips,
My pending orgasm,

I moan,
And you take that as a yes,
Pushing me over the edge
Into oblivion
Little do you know
That oblivion
Is what I crave
Your skin
On my skin
Should be a relief
Not a reminder
Of a memory
I'd rather bury
Under six feet
Of dirt
Along with the rest of me

Not the first time – and not the last

Sometimes
I vomit words
Onto paper
Just to get them
Out of my stomach
When they have me
Doubled over,
Heaving up blood
And other detritus
From the injuries
They left in their wake.
Who knew words
Could be so toxic
When put together
In all the wrong ways,
Telling twisting tales
Of trauma
And fractured glimpses
Of memories
Long since used
As an anesthetic
To make it through
Existence;
Poignant words
For emotions
And paralyzing fears
Haunting the darkest
Parts of me
But maybe, just maybe
If I hurl enough of them
Onto the page,
They'll stop
Poisoning my soul

Some things – I cannot keep inside

A metallic taste
Lingers in the back of my throat
As I walk away
From where you consumed my soul
For your own carnal pleasure.
The alcohol sits warm in my stomach
As I remember your hands
In places they never should've been
Your darkest parts
Gutting me
From the inside out
My stomach threatens to spill its contents
Into the street
Alongside my shame and guilt.
You walked me home from the bar –
A perfect gentleman –
I should have known
Better than that.
I see the swings of the playground,
The slides,
The climbing platform
On which you hollowed me out;
I hear myself begging
"Enough. Please."
"Two more minutes, baby."
As if you ever earned the right to call me baby
Your hands on my thighs,
Keeping me spread open for you.
When you're finished with me
You tell me to stand
"Are you mad at me?"
You ask

Knowing what you did
But only pretending to care.
My insides scream,
And then you left me standing
In the ruins of my innocence
Wondering how I'll ever heal
The junkyard of a body
You discarded and left behind

I shouldn't have been so drunk – and other ways
I blame myself

Blackness exists
Where last night's memories
Should be
Light glints off the shot glasses
In my mind's eye
Whose contents
I poured down my throat
Until there was nothing left to feel;
Drunk on the liquor
But also the numbness, the darkness,
Coming back to consciousness
In a hospital bed and purple gown
The IV in my arm
Aching, throbbing
Like my temples
And the points behind my eyes,
Wishing I were dead
Instead of sobbing
In the darkened bathroom
Next to the trauma bay,
Wishing I were strong enough
To either end or mend my life.
One seems much easier than the other
Like a fireball shot
Goes down much smoother
Than whiskey,
Nearly running
Through the halls
After lying through my teeth
To secure my freedom
"Are you safe?"
"Do you feel better today?"

"Any suicidal thoughts?"
Yes, yes, no
Just tell me
What you need to hear
I'll give you
Anything,
Sprinting,
Wishing I could fly
Faster and faster,
Away from emotion,
Away from reality,
Shutting myself away
Until someone comes to save me,
Though I know no one will

About last night – I'm glad I don't remember

The doctors
Ask me if I'm safe
But how can you know
Anything about safety
If you've never
Felt it?

I can't remember – feeling okay

If nothing else,
I can thank them –
And they know
Who they are,
At least
Most of them do,
And if they don't,
I hope
They burn, burn, burn
The same way
I am scorched
Inside my lungs
From all the breaths
It hurt to take –
For the times
They made me bleed
So I have enough ink
To write away
The parts of me
I cannot bear to keep

I cannot change what happened – but I can let it
make me stronger

Time warps around the edges
When the moon ascends,
Sewn with silver satin
And midnight blue trim.
It folds in on itself –
A Rubik's cube aligning,
Reaching dimensional infinity
With every passing second
Though its passage is meaningless.
I wade through it
As Charon once did
Across the River Styx,
My mind just as full
Of fractured memories,
Deep-set fears,
And shattered dreams.
The morning comes –
Both instantly and hours later –
And I can never be sure
What was lost in the dark
And what was real.
Either way, I know
Night's shimmering gaze
Will fall on me again
Whether I want it to or not

The darkness – is hard to forget

I taste freedom
On my tongue
Sweet but metallic,
A penny coated in sugar.
I am grateful
That this prison
Is no longer mine
To inhabit
But the world outside
Has no plans to change,
And it's only
A matter of time
Before that freedom
Becomes too bitter
To safely consume

Confinement is a form of torture – but so is real
life

I like to say
I am nothing
Like my father,
But when the fury
Roils in my stomach,
Rising from my toes,
Even my heart
Knows to fear
What's coming next

I have a temper – and I am ashamed of it

Sometimes
I wake up starving,
A gnawing ache
In my soul,
Not for food,
Or love,
Or attention,
But for the privilege
Of going back
In time
To show
Each and every one
Of my abusers
That they will not win

I think that past me - would appreciate knowing
there is hope

Part II: Air
On Heartbreak

If only you had told me
That you loved somebody new,
Maybe we could've saved
Part of what we built,
Brick by brick,
But instead you simply
Disappeared,
Leaving the ghost of your touch
On my skin
And the whisper of your voice
In my ears.
And maybe you thought it would be easier,
Maybe you were trying not to hurt me
But it turns out
You shattered me instead

Your absence – almost killed me

She isn't good for me, I know
But that doesn't make me want her less
It doesn't make it easier
To see her with someone new;
To picture his hands in places
Once reserved just for me;
To imagine the laughter
They share when they're alone;
To visit the graveyard
Of what we used to have
And weep at the headstone
Of our love

Cemetery – I'll bring the shovel

No one told me
Forever had an expiration date,
But you knew
And you kept it a secret

Cruel – but I still miss you

While I was ring shopping,
Gauging cut and color,
You were looking for a way out
When all you had to do
Was ask

I'm not a prison warden – just someone who
loved you

How could I have been
So incredibly stupid
To believe
That someone so ashamed
Of every part of me,
So traumatized
By our love
Would ever
Promise forever
And actually mean it

Never good enough – and other lies you told me

You said you loved me,
But you forgot
To tell everyone else

Dirty little secret - did you ever love me at all?

When I asked you
To take me to the stars,
I didn't mean
You should
Drag me to the spaceship's door
And push me toward the Sun

Worlds apart – in every sense of the word

Is it possible
For someone to take up
A negative amount of space,
To be less
Than the air around them?
Anti-matter,
I don't matter;
If I did,
You would've stayed
Instead of stripping me
For the parts you needed most
And scrapping the rest
On your way out,
Condensing me
To less than,
Less than a breath,
A moment,
A passing car
On your highway
When you've always been
My whole journey

Totaled – only twisted metal left

Even as my world
Burned around me,
All I could see
Was the way the flames
Admired your skin

You were the sun – and I had no chance

I thought I knew
Everything about you,
But you were an iceberg
Wrapped in a layer of warmth,
And I was the *Titanic*

Doomed – I needed more lifeboats

Your silence
Hollows me out
More and more
With every passing second,
But if I were to hear your voice
I think that would break me,
So maybe I should appreciate your silence –
Maybe it's an act of mercy after all

A kindness – even if it doesn't feel like it

I've stopped vomiting
When I hear your name,
So I guess
I should get up off the bathroom floor
Or maybe
I'll just sacrifice myself to the plumbing
With your name on my lips

Staring at the bathroom ceiling – sick without
you

I loved you
Like the rain,
All-consuming,
A downpour
Puddling on the streets,
The sidewalks,
Washing away everything else.
I loved you
Like the trees,
Deeply rooted
In growing a life,
A home,
A world for us,
Reaching for the highest highs
But weathering
The harshest winters.
I loved you
Like the city,
Loudly,
Hard,
All square lines
And spotlights
Against an endless horizon.
I loved you
Like tequila shots,
Messily,
Bitterly,
Wanting to feel you
Warm in my stomach,
In my veins,
Poisoning myself
With every touch.

I loved you
Like the summer,
Hot and sticky,
The air thick with wetness
And burnt around the edges,
Almost oppressive
But also dizzying
And free.
I loved you
Like a symphony,
Full,
And soft
In all the right places,
Elegantly
Made of notes,
Tied together
In all the right ways
And sealed
With a standing ovation.
I loved you
Like a hurricane,
Twistingly,
And destructively,
Unstoppable,
Chaos embodied,
Cloaked rage
With a forgiving center.
I loved you
With everything
I had inside of me,
Completely,
Blindly,

Unashamedly.
You loved me
Like a black hole
You took,
And you took,
And you took,
And none of that light
Will ever escape

Like a summer day – or something like that

I cannot say
That you never
Hurt me
When you crushed me
Beneath the weight
Of your silence
After eight long years
Of hearing nothing
But your voice
In my ears
And feeling nothing
But your heartbeat
In my veins

Your pulse became mine – I have no heartbeat
left

Whenever I remember
The good things –
Your hands in my hair
And your smile
Pressed to my forehead,
The clear bell
Of your laugh
And your incorrigible
Sweet tooth,
All of the things
I took for granted
When I called you mine –
I find myself
Stepping into traffic
And hoping I don't
Make it across

Even if I die – my love for you won't

I wish we had never taken
All of those photos –
The one of you looking
At me
The one of you looking
At the stars
Soft smiles, wide grins
Sweaters
Snow
Brunch
The black romper
I would've married you in
If you had let me
The red dress
That looked just as beautiful
On the floor
Freckles
Green eyes
Long, dark hair
"Hey! Smile!"
I wish you hadn't listened
I wish you would've stopped me
But looking at you
Was a drug
And my camera
Sustained my high
Hot chocolate in the park
Vineyards
Birthdays
New Years
"Should I post it?"
Of course I'd post you

Over and over
I'd like it a thousand times
If I could
Videos of you dancing, singing
In the car
On the bus
In the rain
The only soundtracks
I'd play on repeat
I wish we had never taken
All of those photos
Erasing them
Feels like I'm losing you
All over again

Old photographs – and other mistakes we made

Sometimes
I see you in places
You've never been
A crowded plaza in Williamsburg
Where you asked me
If I wanted to live with you;
A plane bound for Europe –
I let you have the window seat
Even though my name was on the ticket –
An adoption center
For rescue animals,
Your smile too wide
To deny you any dog you wanted;
In my bed,
Looking at me
Like I am oxygen
And you are suffocating,
Vulnerable and open,
So clearly in love,
Drunk,
Intoxicated,
High on being together,
Weaving our lives into one
As if it were the most natural thing,
As if it was fated.
I don't believe in fate,
But I believed in you,
And that was my first mistake.
That's when
I see you in places
We've been before –
Angry, proud

Saying things we don't mean,
Throwing words like rocks,
Promising each other
Things we could never
Ever
Hope to achieve;
Forever
Spelled out in the stitches
Used to sew up
The wounds
On our hearts
From nights left alone,
Empty, apart
Codependent, needy
Two hydrogen atoms, one oxygen
Bound together
To sustain life,
But still we were lost in the desert
And dying of thirst.
We were poison.
Toxic,
Yet we consumed each other
Like we were starving,
Indifferent
To the possibility of death,
A skull and crossbones –
The symbol of our love –
Desperate to feel you
Next to me,
Inside me,
All around me,
Engulfing me

Making me feel,
Like you ever loved me at all
Did you?
Don't answer that.
Sometimes
It's better not to know,
Sometimes
I see you in places
You've never been,
And every time
I wish we had more time
And that goodbye
Wasn't the only thing left
To say
But I'll keep talking
To your memory
And hope that one day
You'll stop lingering
In places
I no longer
Wish you had been

Everywhere – even when I wish you were
nowhere

I love you,
I love you,
I love you
If I say it three times,
Spin around
In a circle,
Cross my heart
And hope to die,
Drink water
Upside down,
Hop on one foot
For two minutes,
Knock on the mirror
With the lights off,
And scream your name
Until I cry,
Will you come back?

I'm trying not to beg – but I will if I need to

Part III: Fire
On Pain

You throw the word
"Broken"
Around like
A frisbee, a baseball,
Recreationally,
Carelessly,
Oblivious
To the bruises
Left on my heart
Each time
You throw it
In my direction

Fun and games – until it isn't

Numb
To everything
Except the letters
Swirling in my brain,
Pulling words
From places I didn't know existed,
Describing emotions
I didn't know I could feel,
Inking them on my skin
Permanent,
Irreversible,
So I remember how it felt
To be at rock bottom,
Clawing at the walls
To come up for air.
I am bent,
Trying not to break
Counting on the words
To catch me
When I fall

Standing on a dictionary – to be one step up
from rock bottom

Inking the words on my arms
I could never say aloud
Makes the burden a little lighter,
Makes me a little stronger,
Investing in a future
Previously unseen,
Unbelievable,
Fractures in a magic mirror
Reflecting
Fissures in my own armor,
My own soul
"Doesn't it hurt?"
They ask
But what they don't know
Is how much I crave the pain
How much pain I've already carved
Onto my body
At least this is art
Where I created only chaos
On the canvas of my skin
Black ink
To cover the darkness
"Won't people judge you?"
They ask
Maybe they will,
But I'd rather have a life
To be judged
Than have no life at all,
Ended with an act of violence,
Falling on my own sword
But without the honor
Of a samurai

"Those are permanent you know"
They say
So are scars
And the ghosts
That haunt the places we call home;
Forever
Is only as long as your breathing lasts,
And when I'm gone
Will they remember
The images on my arms?
The things I cared enough about
To etch them on my skin?
Or will they remember
An idealized version
Of the body I was forced to inhabit
Until the bitter end
"I could never get a tattoo"
They say
"Then don't"
I answer
But I did,
And I will keep getting them
Until I feel like the outside matches
The marring on the inside –
How else will you see
That I'm drowning?

Permanence – and other false states of being

Broken and beautiful
Are not
Mutually exclusive terms,
So stop telling me
I am broken
Unless you have seen
Just how beautifully
The pieces of me
Shatter

Broken windows – still let the light in

Hurtling toward the sun
At the speed of light
On a rocket with no brakes,
No reverse,
Full throttle
Into the panic,
Letting reality slip away.
Close your eyes
And hold on tight
Until you can't anymore

Letting go – the more attractive option

I've always wondered
What it feels like to drown,
But then I think
Of all the moments,
All of the emotional capital
I've spent
Trying to explain
How desperately I want to die,
How much it hurts to live,
How incredibly alone I feel,
And then I know
I've felt it all along

2 minutes – how long I can hold my breath

The saddest
I have ever felt
Was when the question
"What will make me happy?"
Turned into
"How much longer can I do this?"

Tomorrows – they are never guaranteed

Just when I think
The pit in my stomach
Can't possibly
Grow any bigger,
Something happens
That has me bent over a toilet,
Choking on remorse and humiliation,
Desperate to exorcise
My apology to the world
For existing

I'm sorry – I hate myself too

Maybe I wield
My poetry
Like a sledgehammer
So I can break something
Besides my own spirit

I'm sorry – if I'm breaking your heart instead

I used to think
That the street
Was reserved only
For walking, riding, driving,
But now I find myself
Whispering my secrets
To the pavement
And wetting the asphalt
With my tears
More often than anything else

Best friends with the ground – it's less far to fall

I feel too much,
Too quick,
Too real,
A flash flood
Of regret and anger,
A reel of mistakes
Played on an endless loop
Bringing bile to the back of my throat,
Burning on the way up,
Ravaging the darkness
With demons
That only I can see;
Like Atlas laboring
Under the weight of the world,
My own shoulders are collapsing
Under the crushing feeling
Of reality,
Of everythingeverywhereeverysecond,
Paralyzed from head to toe.
By all accounts
I should be broken, beaten,
Huddled in a puddle of tears
And I truly want nothing more
Than to lay down
And scream, weep
But the most ironic part of all
Is that I can't even cry

Dry eyes – and other false flags

Choking on the glitter
Shoved down my throat each June
Bones cracking, heart breaking
Under the weight of the words
"I'm gay"
Lungs filling up with blood
Drowning, gasping to the rhythm
Of the words
"I'm sick"
But you don't look sick
"I'm the type of sick you can't see"
Spinal column folding in on itself
Ankles too weak to stand
Under the neon sign
Flashing "broken"
Above my head
In bold, rainbow colors
Stripped naked, bare
In front of the mirror
Anger, rage
Boiling up from my stomach
And into my throat
Microscopic cracks form in the glass
The thrown object lying innocently
On the floor
But maybe the reflection
Is more accurate now,
Punctuated by scars and imperfections
From trying to cut away
All of the broken parts
And watch them run down my arms,
Blood red and bitter,

Filled to the brim with self-hatred,
Flashes of memory
Glimpsed in the glass,
Begging for mercy
From someone bigger and stronger
Than my eight year old frame,
The bogeyman haunting my dreams
Violent, looming
I'm older now
But the bogeyman is still here
Turns out
After all of this time,
After all of this running,
The bogeyman has become me

My own worst enemy – and other hard
realizations

There is nothing
Quite like
The high you get
From dragging a blade
Across your skin
And watching the blood
Spell out your pain
In its bright red
Cursive

I don't do drugs – but there are other ways to get

I keep crossing out
The words I put
To the page,
Hoping something brighter
Will take the place
Of the barbed wire
I refuse to stomach
Any longer

Praying for the best – expecting the worst

Yesterday I felt
Like I was walking on air
It is almost unbelievable
How quickly the oxygen
Became molten lead,
Burning the bottoms
Of my soles
And coating the inside
Of my lungs.
I wish it were
Just as easy
To make that transformation
In reverse,
But I bet not even
The Philosopher's Stone
Could perform such complex
Alchemical miracles,
Not even magic
Could make this burden
Simply disappear.
I should just let it
Crush me,
But I know they'd try
To resurrect me
And force me
To turn this poison
Into wine,
But they don't understand
That they should not
Worship at my altar,

I am not a martyr
Or a saint –
I am just someone
Who Fortune forgot
And left behind

Unlucky – is my middle name

"How are you?"
A question asked in passing
With a scripted answer
"I'm fine. How are you?"
A mirrored response,
But what if I were honest
For once?
What if I told you
How dark my thoughts are?
What if I told you
I cut my own skin
And watch the blood run down my arms
To make myself feel better?
Would you run away?
I wouldn't blame you –
I spend my days
Trying to run away from myself,
But you're the lucky one
I can't escape
But you can leave
Just like everyone else

Alone – with my own worst enemy

A heart
Blackened by fire
And shattered by grief
Still feels;
The ocean
Darkened by storms
And ravaged by wind
Still soothes;
The most intimate
Of relationships,
Of friendships,
Of love
Are tested time and again,
After heaving ugly, bitter words
Around and around –
But gorgeous apologies
Flowered and serifed,
And tied with a cursive bow
Mend the ragged wounds
From such careless whispers
And broken promises,
Healed scars becoming
Thin white lines,
Mirroring the drugs
Used to forget the past,
An intoxicating high
Coupled with haunting addiction,
Hopes and dreams,
The limitless possibility
Of a future undetermined,
But suddenly
Crushed by circumstance

Or spite –
Is nothing more debilitating?
Until the seeds
Of new hope are sown,
And light blooms once more;
The conundrum of the coexistence
And codependence,
Of our happiest moments
And greatest fears
Walking the same line
Lives in no man's land,
Too confusing for our minds
To make sense of
But too attractive
Of an idea to ignore;
Excitement bubbling
At the very thought
Of a world without
Ugliness, brutality,
Focusing only on the beauty
But who's to say that beauty
Isn't the most brutal thing of all

Black and white – but living in all of the gray
areas

A string of keys
Hangs from the ceiling –
No locks,
No chains –
But I'm lying underneath,
Hoping someone will come along
And use them to open
All the doors
I've closed,
And all the windows
I've shut
To keep the world away
From my center,
To protect myself
From the inevitability
Of more damage

Open me up – but leave me broken

I envy Eve,
The thief of forbidden fruit,
The cause of our eviction
From Eden, from paradise.
Even if she's remembered
As a villain,
Even if she was in pain,
At least her mistake
Was her own,
While I am Abel, Seth, and Cain
Cast down to Earth,
Subject to agony
And damned by an original sin
That was not my own

I may not be a saint – but not everything is my
fault

Oscar Wilde once said,
"The books that the world
Calls immoral
Are books that show the world
Its own shame."
Can that not be said
Of people too?

Are you ashamed of me? – banished to the psych
ward

The fact that
A scientist
Can distill
Mental illness
Down to a chemical formula,
A list
Of causes,
Of societal factors
Queer, black, brown, female, transgender, sick,
disabled, gay, lesbian, autistic, other
Is a reflection
Of what they fear,
Not of us

If I say it enough times – I might just believe it

Come out
With us
To dance,
To drink too much,
To live
Just a little.
Come out
To visit,
A road trip
Or a flight
To someone
I haven't seen
In far too long.
Come out
To play,
The neighbor kids
Banging on the front door
With a basketball
In hand.
"Come out, come out
Wherever you are!"
The seeker shouts
After counting
To one hundred
But inevitably
Skipping some numbers
Along the way.
Let's go see
That movie
When it
Comes out,
The trailer looked

Compelling.
Coming out
Can mean
A thousand things
But it will always
Mean nothing to me
But my silent curse
Of having to say
Over and over again
"I'm gay"

Coming out – and other societal obscenities

I am measured in accomplishments;
I am marked by pride;
I am defined by success
Until
I'm checking the disability box
And disclosing –
Exposing –
My failure
Of body and mind

Unfit for capitalism – caught in the in-between

There's something kind of beautiful
In the dark,
In the ugly,
In the pain.
Isn't it funny
That without the bad
There could be no good?
And to me
That's a little poetic,
Even if it hurts

Funny – except I'm not laughing

Poetry
Is supposed to be beautiful,
Full of sunny adjectives
And well-placed prepositions,
Rhyming couplets
Describing clouds and the rain,
Love and loss,
Similes and metaphors
Likening nature to life
Or something simple
To something wonderful.
So why is it
That when I try to write,
Darkness
Falls onto the page
And fire burns the edges,
Singeing the words,
Burdening the lines
With the sheer weight
Of the emotions
That I could never express
In any other way;
Sketching images
Of death, war, sickness
With my words,
Sharing the onus
I can't carry on my own –
Staccato stanzas
Damaged at best,
Shattered at worst.
Poetry
Is supposed to be beautiful,
So why is my poetry
More like a call for help

Nothing but darkness – heartache is my muse

There is a potent
Type of pain
That comes from
Being lonely –
A walking on hot coals
Type of burning,
A box cutter to the vein
Type of agony,
A haymaker to the throat
Type of asphyxiation –
And so we find ourselves
Drowning
Bits and pieces of our being
In the brush of a hand
From a stranger on the street
And the subsequent, "Sorry";
The energy of a crowd
On the train platform,
A drug,
Habit-forming and addictive;
The "good morning"
From a favorite barista
A masterpiece
To play on repeat;
These tiny windows
Into a world
In which we are forgetting
How to be kind
To each other,
How to love first
And judge second,

Far from the trust
And harmony
And order
Of our hunter and gatherer
Ancestors.
I think that people
Are mostly good;
I need to believe
That people
Are mostly good –
Otherwise,
Do we have anything
To fight for?
Anyone
To die for?
They say that
To err is human,
But they never
Talk about
How desperately
Wanting to be loved
And wanting to love
In return
Is the most human
Thing of all.
There is a special
Kind of agony
That comes from
Being lonely
In this harsh existence,
And I'm waiting
For us to remember,

Collectively,
How much better it is
To be together
In the trenches
Instead of ruling
Over an island of pride
And hatred
All alone

I want to believe that people are mostly good
– but they always prove me wrong

About the Author

Hayley Lazzari is an author and poet. She lives in Brooklyn, New York with her roommates, and her dog, Bex (who is her whole heart). When not writing, she likes to read, do crosswords ("I am a proud cruciverbalist") and play puzzle games. She also enjoys going to the gym and walking her dog.

Milton Keynes UK
Ingram Content Group UK Ltd.
UKHW010730231023
431165UK00001B/47